# farting

## with Vimrod

# farting

my farts
hospitalise
small
children

Vimrod by Lisa Swerling and Ralph Lazar

HarperCollins*Entertainment*
*An Imprint of HarperCollinsPublishers*

if i was
**queen**
for a
day,

i would spend that day
**naked** but wearing
my **crown**, i would bathe
in warm **milk** and
**fart**
a lot

# life is short

**fart in elevators**

# i am a woman

but by golly my farts are
## masculine

do
fish
fart?

what's that **smell?**

oh, hello.

# graduate, royal college of fine fart

nice one

in life, fart transmitters
tend to be more successful
than fart receivers.

which are you?

# my new mobile phone has inbuilt fart-detection capability

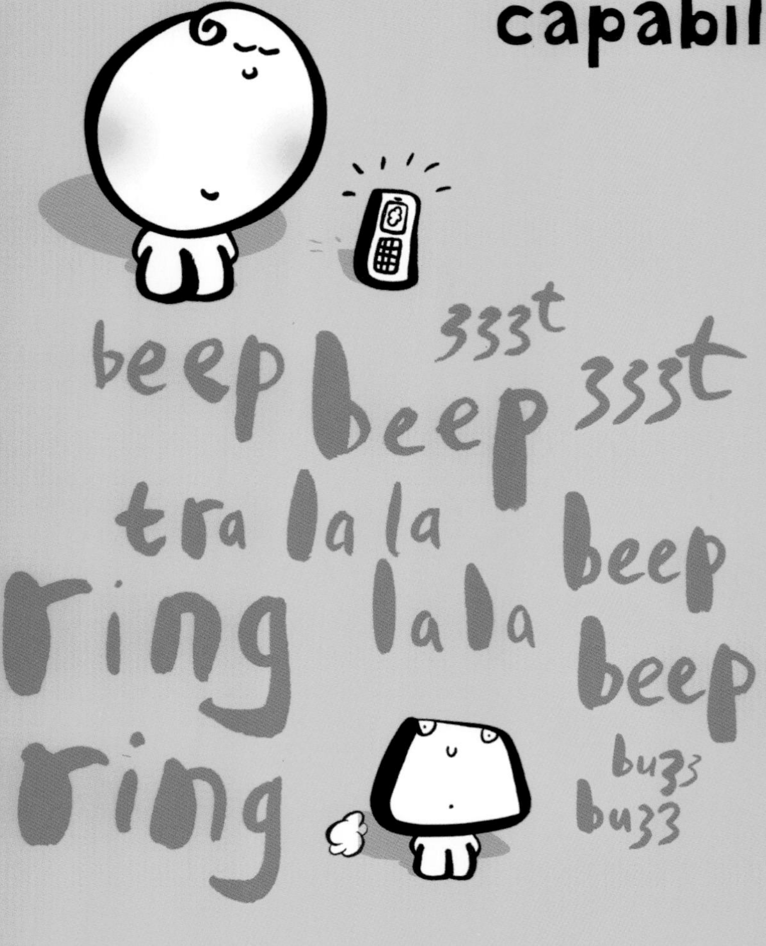

my farts are so impressive
that I have hired an **agent**

# i love you,
### except when
### you're upwind

# tick appropriate category:

☐ **loud but proud**

"phfrtt"

☐ silent but **violent**

did you know that
every time you fart
you lose **0.001% of**
*your* **brain?**

good news.
i've declared a
## cease-fart.

and on the

eighth day

god
farted

if farting were taxed
you'd be in
serious
trouble

the farting cheshire cat
faded away until all
that was left was the...

...oh no, that's

gross

are you smiling because you're happy

or because you've just made a little fart?

**lisa swerling + ralph lazar**

are two of the UK's most familiar
graphic artists. Through their company
Last Lemon they have spawned a catwalk
of popular cartoon characters, which
includes Harold's Planet, The Brainwaves,
Blessthischick and, of course, Vimrod.

writers, artists and designers, they are
married with two children, and spend
their time between London and various
beaches on the Indian Ocean.

- - - - - - - - - - - - - - - - - - - - - - - - - - - - - - - - - - - - - - - - - -

HarperCollins*Entertainment*
An Imprint of HarperCollins*Publishers*
77–85 Fulham Palace Road, Hammersmith, London W6 8JB

www.harpercollins.co.uk

Published by HarperCollins*Entertainment* 2006
3

A catalogue record for this book is available from the British Library

ISBN-10   0 00 723416 3
ISBN-13   978 0 00 723416 5

Set in Bokka
Printed and bound in Italy by Lego SpA

other titles in the **Vimrod** collection:

(watch this space)